BUSINESS
C · A · R · D
DESIGN

Donna E. Hicks
Book Design: Mark A. Hicks

ART DIRECTION BOOK COMPANY
NEW YORK

2nd Printing 1991
© Copyright 1989, Art Direction Book Co.

Library of Congress Catalog Card Number: 89-80317

ISBN: 088108-066-7

Art Direction Book Company
10 East 39th Street
New York, N.Y. 10016
Printed in Singapore

C·O·N·T·E·N·T·S

P·R·E·F·A·C·E

The most useful kind of business card book would be one with actual business cards attached in it. That not being possible, this book was created as the next best option.

This book serves as a showcase for well-designed cards, while at the same time breaking the business card into its separate elements of copy, art, design, type, paper, and ink and discussing each of these aspects. The goal of this book is to make the process of putting all these elements together much easier with the resulting cards more appealing.

I gratefully acknowledge the assistance of my husband, Mark, who not only designed this book but also helped with the writing and editing.

T·H·E
COPY

It is quite likely, in fact highly probable, that no business card will ever be considered a literary masterpiece. Still, that does not negate the importance of the business card's words.

Unfortunately, most business card copy is written according to a finished layout, with words being chosen not on their function but on their fit. Or the words are taken straight off of an old card, without any thought as to what should be added or what could be deleted.

In creating a business card, however, writing the copy should be one of the first steps. It should be done carefully, with the specific purpose of the card in mind.

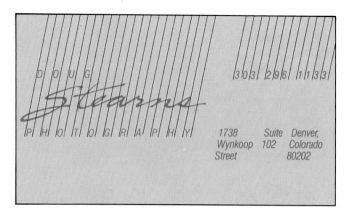

A business card should tell a potential customer all that's needed. The Doug Stearns Photography card presents the basic information—name, address, and phone number—and in a creative manner.

Designed by: Unit 1, Inc.

Management Technology International, Inc.
Computer Based Management Systems

One Greentree Centre   **Joe Cunningham**
Marlton, New Jersey 08053   District Sales Manager
(609) 596-4355

Here, the four-word business description is unneeded for regular customers but useful to prospective clients. It is set under the full company name in 6 point, the smallest type on the card.

Designed by: Unit 1, Inc.

TELELINK

Business
Telephone
Systems

TeleLink Corporation
125 Frontage Road
Orange, CT 06477-3604
203/795-1200

Business Telephone Systems is the concise company description for TeleLink. Quotation marks are not necessary around descriptions or mottos.

Designed by: Pappas & MacDonnell

Norman J. Giem, P.E.
Consulting Engineer

Consultant for power generation, gas turbines and steam turbines. Project management, engineering, review, inspection and start-up.

P.O. Box 1240
Koloa, Hawaii 96756
Phone: (808) 742-9726
or (808) 335-6251
Telex: RCA 723-8450
Ans. back: 8450 TELEX HR

Two equal length sentences with no unnecessary words describe GIEM's business. The long copy is more readable in the narrow 8-pica width, as opposed to being set the whole width of the card. The narrow copy block also helps to balance the logo above it.

Designed by: Goodson + Yu Design

Instead of giving a business description, the Bay East Graphics card lists the company's services. This is a good technique to use when all the services can be included; otherwise, the list can be limiting.

Designed by: Gene Russell, Bay East Graphics

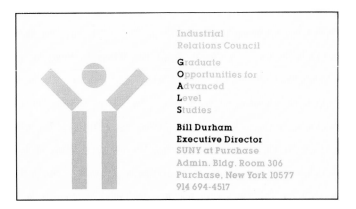

Here, the description under the council's name includes an acronym that is read vertically. *GOALS* and the director's name and title are in black. The rest of the card is in gray.

Designed by: Salpeter Paganucci, Inc.

Bruce Hands uses only his first name above the company title, his full name. Both are in the same type and size.

The small amount of type gives emphasis to the illustration. The hands symbolize the photographer's last name, and the sleeves represent film.

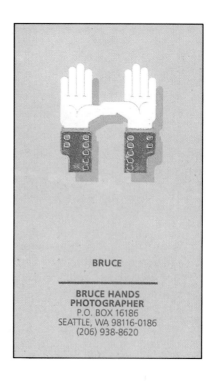

Designed by: Jack Anderson and Cliff Chung, Hornall Anderson Design Works

Sandy Cowen's card is another way to handle a personal name that is the same as the company name. Creative humor is effective on cards if it matches the company's or employee's personality.

Designed by: Sandy Cowen Agency Inc.

Though a title on a business card is not mandatory, listing the department or field in which the employee works is, in most cases, useful. On this card, James Curley's title of *Vice President* is followed by his department, *Sales/Marketing*.

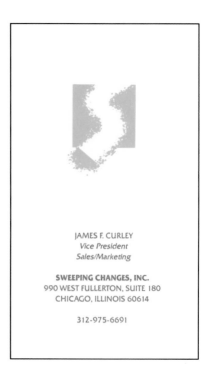

JAMES F. CURLEY
Vice President
Sales/Marketing

SWEEPING CHANGES, INC.
990 WEST FULLERTON, SUITE 180
CHICAGO, ILLINOIS 60614

312-975-6691

Designed by: Michael Stanard, Inc.

Well-known titles and degrees can be abbreviated, but those that are not self-explanatory should be spelled out or explained.

On this card, *Family Practice* is centered under *Gary A. Nussey, M.D.* When a degree or title follows a name on the same line, a comma is needed.

Designed by: Potts & Plans

Dr. Helmut Meyer
Developmental Research

QuantM Corporation
Denningerstrasse 198/5 D-8000
Munchen 81
(089) 93 33 00

An employee name at the top of a card or in any other prominent location can signify, however subtly, a valued employee. Here a corporation in Germany has the employee's name and title above the logo and separate from its name and address.

Designed by: John Hornall, Jack Anderson, and Andrea Sames, Hornall Anderson Design Works

Henry Less
Producer/Director

Henry Less Productions Inc.
1196 Queen Street West
Toronto, Ontario M6J 1J6
(416) 532-1116

If a company has more than one employee, its card design should accommodate employee names of various lengths. On the Henry Less Productions card, a change from a short name to a longer name would not disturb the design.

Designed by: Henry Less Productions Inc.

Thomas J. Stewart
Chief Executive Officer
Residence: (206) 463-3269

3415 11th Avenue SW
Seattle, WA 98134
(206) 623-0304

**Services Group
of America**

Home phone numbers and numbers that ring directly to an employee's office are normally listed close to the employee's name. General office numbers are usually listed near the company address. For clarification, *Residence* precedes this top number.

Designed by: Jack Anderson and Juliet Shen, Hornall Anderson Design Works

Since Earlybird does not conduct business through the mail, no address is listed on the card, only telephone numbers and telex number.

Designed by: Duk Engelhardt and Evan Gross, DesignInk

martha a. bogdanoff
2248 n. gower
hollywood, ca.
90068
(213) 462-3796

The use of all lowercase letters produces a creative look for this art director's card. This unconventional style would not be successful, however, for all professions.

Designed by: Martha A. Bogdanoff

Lisa Murphy

1156 Shure Dr., Suite 310
Arlington Heights, IL 60004
312-392-3992

Simple, bare minimum copy makes for easy readability. *Telephone* is not printed before the phone number, parentheses around the area code are deleted, and the state is abbreviated in the two letter form.

Designed by: LMG Communications

Abbreviations can shorten an address, allowing it to be set larger. The address on Kim Freilich's card is abbreviated so that it fits in an 8-point line under the logo. Ample room is left between the address and phone number, set bold.

Designed by: Thom Dower

MECHANICALS INSIDE

30 EAST 21 STREET • 2B • NEW YORK, NY 10010 • (212) 505-2570

MECHANICALS
PHOTOSTATS
TYPOGRAPHY

JOHN SALAYI

Bullets, in lieu of commas, are used to separate items in this card's address. Bullets work well here, as commas and most other punctuation marks do not reproduce well in small reverse type.

Designed by: John Salayi, Inside Mechanicals

7800 E. Iliff,
Suite E
Denver, Colorado 80231
(303) 369-9530

Steve Wilson
President

Colorado
Land
Consultants, Inc.

Land Surveying/Engineering

Here, abbreviations and line breaks enhance the design. *East* is abbreviated in the first line of the address to make the line close to the same length as the first line of the company name, set below. The second line in the address is about the same length as *Land*, the second line in the company name. In the third address line, the state name is spelled out so that the line parallels the third line of the company name.

Designed by: Unit 1, Inc.

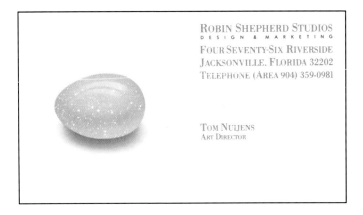

The street address is spelled out on this card so that the line is the same length as the other copy lines. Also, the last line is made longer with *Telephone* and *Area.*

This is the company's formal card, which is given to corporate clients. The company's informal card is shown on page 130.

Designed by: Tom Nuijens, Robin Shepherd Studios

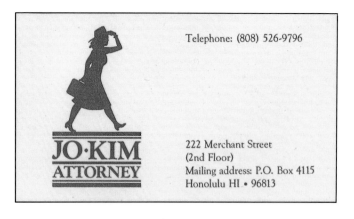

Telephone: (808) 526-9796

JO·KIM
ATTORNEY

222 Merchant Street
(2nd Floor)
Mailing address: P.O. Box 4115
Honolulu HI • 96813

The address on Jo Kim's card includes the street address, a description of the location, and a mailing address. The city, state, and zip code are not repeated since they are the same for both addresses.

Designed by: Goodson + Yu Design

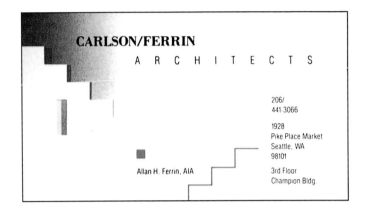

Here, a description of the business location is set under the complete address. This way, the description is emphasized and will not be mistaken as being part of the actual address.

Designed by: Jack Anderson, Hornall Anderson Design Works

Julie Nurré
Assistant General Manager

(808) 834-7666
Telex: 333593
FAX: (808) 833-4627

H E M M E T E R • A V I A T I O N

Honolulu • Maui • Kona • Hilo • Kauai

Honolulu International Airport
98 Kapalulu Place
Honolulu, Hawaii 96819

The Hemmeter Aviation card includes, along with its address, all the places in which the company does business. The locations are listed directly under the logo but in smaller type than the address.

Designed by: Goodson + Yu Design

T·H·E
ART

Just as the copy on a business card should serve a purpose, so also should the art. The purpose of the art might be to reveal information about the company's products and services or portray the company's style. It may be to increase the card's readability or make the card more attractive.

In order to serve its purpose, however, the art—whether it's a logo, photo, rule, or other graphic element—needs to look good within the confines of a 2 x 3 1/2 inch card. And that's not always as simple as it seems.

Eden Foods, Inc.   517-456-7424
701 Tecumseh Road   313-973-9400
Clinton, Michigan   FAX 517-456-7025
U.S.A.   49236   TWX 510-450-5400

Martha S. Johnson
Marketing Manager

The small logo on the Eden Foods card produces a formal appearance. A horizontal layout is created through the use of equally-sized blocks placed side by side.

Designed by: Group 243 Inc.

Hair By
Bellingham Towers
Suite 480
(206) 647-1766

The large logo on this card gives a bold, creative statement. Hair by Chaplin is located in Bellingham, Washington.

Designed by: Modern Dog Design

The iguana logo takes up half of the card but does not overpower the restaurant name. Running the iguana and the rules in the same color—turquoise—helps to blend the art with the logotype, which is in maroon. The turquoise and maroon ink create a Southwestern look.

Designed by: Duk Engelhardt and Evan Gross, DesignInk

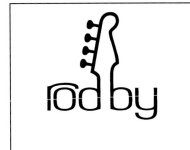

STEVE RODBY
ELECTRIC AND ACOUSTIC BASS

STEVE RODBY
ACOUSTIC AND ELECTRIC BASS

Two different logos are used on Steve Rodby's card—one on each side. The bass player is equally adept at acoustic and electric bass, hence the two designs. No phone number or address is included due to his traveling with a musical group.

Designed by: Michael Waitsman, Synthesis Concepts Incorporated

DAVID ROMAN
Branch Manager

11027 North 24th Avenue, Suite 704
Phoenix, Arizona 85029
602/246-4211
800/352-5417
For Supplies: 800/DIAL-GBC

Here, two logos are incorporated on a one-sided card. The bottom logo balances rather than competes with the main logo. Both *GBC*'s are in red, with the type and box in brown.

Designed by: GBC

A statement of the photographer's style and skill is given through the black-and-white photo on this card. The card size is 2 1/2 x 3 1/2 inches.

Designed by: George Kavanagh

The two rules help to blend the logo with the type. The top of the company name is aligned with the top of the logo. The last address line is flush with the bottom of the logo.

Designed by: Phil Otto, Image Design

CHANGE FOR GOOD

2439 Ontario Road, NW
Washington, DC 20009

202/328-6922

David Barker, *Executive Director*

The three 1 point rules running the width of the card reinforce the horizontal design. They parallel the three reverse rules in the coins. The company is a not-for-profit group which collects foreign currency and applies it to public service community projects.

Designed by: Lisa Marks-Ellis, Synthesis Concepts Incorporated

The 9 point type is centered between the five rules. Descenders are not considered since there are none in the all-capital style. Cheryl Yuen is a fine arts development consultant.

Designed by: Mike Mulligan, Synthesis Concepts Incorporated

CHERYL YUEN

312 MALDEN
LA GRANGE PARK
ILLINOIS 60525
312 / 352 - 2548

Herbert N. Conley
President

CONLEY DEW

333 Queen Street • Suite 710
Honolulu, Hawaii 96813

(808) 524-2844
FAX (808) 521-7300

Different-sized rules in different colors enhance the
Conley Dew card. The line under the logotype is about
the same thickness as the letters of the type, a good rule
about rules to follow when underlining type.

Designed by: Goodson + Yu Design

Susan Spivack

Graphic Design

119 West 23rd Street

New York, NY 10011

212-924-4453

The screened rules do not overpower the type. The rules bleed off both sides of the card, lining up with the rules on the back. The letterhead and envelopes are designed similarly.

Designed by: Susan Spivack Graphic Design

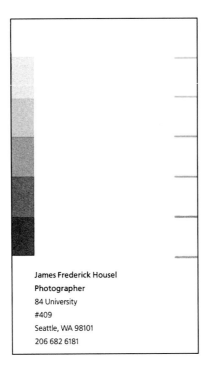

James Frederick Housel
Photographer
84 University
#409
Seattle, WA 98101
206 682 6181

This photographer's card has a simulated gray scale running down the left side. The number of copy lines is the same as the number of rules on the right.

Designed by: Jack Anderson and Raymond Terada, Hornall Anderson Design Works

Drafting symbols are printed in light gold in the background. The logo and type are placed strategically around the art.

Designed by: Jack Anderson and Jani Drewfs, Hornall Anderson Design Works

Type, rules, dots, a solid block, and a screen block are scattered across the card but linked together by design. The employee name lines up under the company name. The address is flush with the left end of the solid block.

Designed by: Tom Dolle Design

An alignment of type and art pulls this design together also. The logotype lines up with the rectangle below it, and the top three lines of type are aligned with the three cut-out edges on the art to the left.

Designed by: Brad Copeland, Copeland Design, Incorporated

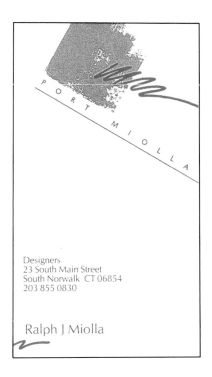

Designers
23 South Main Street
South Norwalk CT 06854
203 855 0830

Ralph J Miolla

The zigzag line which bleeds off the top edge of this card appears again at the bottom.

For most cards with bleeds, a printer will need to make extra cuts.

Designed by: Port Miolla

The rules bleeding off both sides give the art on this card a continuity—as if the art continues on past the card. The rules and the logotype are in light brown ink, and the rest of the card is in dark brown.

Designed by: Goodson + Yu Design

EDDIE CELNICK
CELNICK/EKSTEIN STUDIO INC.
36 EAST 12 STREET
NEW YORK CITY 10003
(212) 420-9326

REPRESENTED BY
SHOOTING STARS
(212) 473-4455

Two solid purple rectangles bleed off both ends of this card. The block on top is the width of the longest line of type. The block on the bottom is the width of the logo.

Designed by: Duk Engelhardt, DesignInk

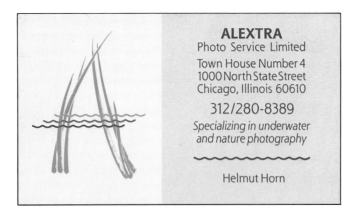

The 5 percent blue screen behind the blue type gives an underwater effect. On the *A* logo, the blades of grass are green, and the three waves are in three different shades of blue.

Designed by: Lisa Marks-Ellis, Synthesis Concepts Incorporated

A mezzotint screen is used on this logotype so that the letters appear as if they were made from clay. The light brown, clay-colored ink reinforces this illusion.

Designed by: Lisa Marks-Ellis, Synthesis Concepts Incorporated

A 150-line, 10 percent screen provides the background for this card. The address and screened dots, printed in orange, are burned into the screen.

Designed by: Thom Dower

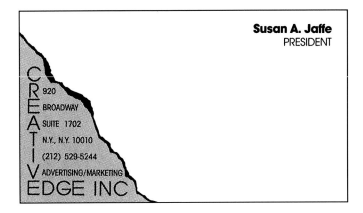

The left corner of this card appears to be torn off, revealing the "Creative Edge." The screen is 110-line, 30 percent.

Designed by: Lisa A. Speroni and Susan Jaffe, Creative Edge Inc.

DONAIS
DIAGNOSTIC
DIMENSIONS

Paul A. Donais, Ph.D.
32 Chestnut Hill Road
Glastonbury, Connecticut 06033
203 · 633 · 3096

Executive Assessment
Management Development
Career Reassessment

A graduated dot screen is used on the front and back of this 2 3/8 x 4 inch card. The company name is reversed into the screen on the front.

Designed by: Susan Spivack Graphic Design

T · H · E
DESIGN

The design of a business card should meet several criteria:

—Since a business card receives only a glance, the design must communicate information quickly and clearly.

—The design should complement the company's image and appeal to the company's clients or customers;

—The card should blend with the company's letterhead and envelopes.

—The design must look good not just in the comp stage but in the final, printed form—working in concert with the card's typeface, paper, and ink.

PET MEDIC ™

Pet Medic Corporation
996 Main Street
Evanston, Illinois 60202
312/869 9828

Distribution Center
8250 South Akron Street Suite 205
Englewood, Colorado 80112
303/790 1655

Pet Medic Corporation
966 Main Street
Evanston, Illinois 60202
312 869 9828

PET MEDIC ™

The Pet Medic cards portray how similar elements can be effectively arranged on a vertical or horizontal layout, with the logo on the top or the bottom of the card.

Designed by: Michael Stanard, Inc.

Unit 1, Inc.   Chuck Danford
Graphic Design

1556 Williams Street
Denver, Colorado 80218
303/320-1116

The card has a symmetrical balance, with the company
name and employee name balancing one another and
the logotype and address doing the same. The logotype
is blind embossed on the actual card but is printed here
in black.

Designed by: Unit 1, Inc.

JOHN P. KNUTSON

Business :

Route 7
Pine Point Road
Menomonie, Wisconsin 54751
715-235-6169

Graphics One

Residence:
715-235-6040

The logo on the right is offset by the copy on the left. The ample white space draws attention to the logo.

Designed by: John P. Knutson, Graphics One

Water Tower Place
835 North Michigan Avenue
Chicago, Illinois 60611
312 943 2050

Karen DeFilippi

Here, the copy is as high over the *Over the Rainbow* logo as possible. The employee name is dropped exactly one line below the phone number.

Designed by: Michael Stanard, Inc.

News & Sports Summaries for the Hawaiian-at-Heart

Lynette Lo Tom
President
Update Productions, Inc.

P.O. Box 22357
Honolulu, Hawaii 96822
(808) 537-4491, 531-6398

With the bottom copy flush left and right, white space is allowed into the center of the card under the nameplate-like logo, giving the card some breathing room.

Designed by: Goodson + Yu Design

RALSTON
PHOTOGRAPHY

P.O. Box 7203
Seattle, WA
98133
206·624·9110

SALLY
RUSSELL

The tripod is placed on the "floor" of the card. The type in the upper right corner offsets the logo.

Designed by: Jack Anderson and Cheri Huber, Hornall Anderson Design Works

Here, the logo is not flush against the bottom edge of the card; instead, white space is allowed under the art. Robert K. Miller is a slight-of-hand magician.

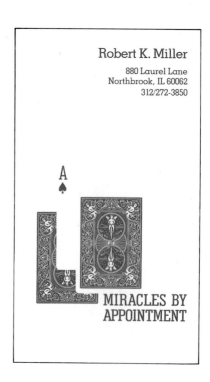

Robert K. Miller

880 Laurel Lane
Northbrook, IL 60062
312/272-3850

A
♠

MIRACLES BY
APPOINTMENT

Designed by: Michael Waitsman, Synthesis Concepts Incorporated

**Eagle Pacific
Insurance Company**

Lawrence R. Hoehne
Chairman, CEO

1450
Fourth & Blanchard Bldg.
Seattle, WA 98121
(206) 441-6636

On this clean layout, the eagle logo, facing toward the type, is centered top to bottom. The top of the employee's name is even with the top of the eagle's wings. The eagle is embossed in purple, with the marks under the eagle in varying shades of blue.

Designed by: Jack Anderson and Raymond Terada, Hornall Anderson Design Works

JCPenney

Vincent R. Sauchelli
Catalog Art Services Manager

J.C. Penney Company, Inc. 1301 Avenue of the Americas
New York, N.Y. 10019, Tel. 212-957-3965

Logo and type are flush left on this card, creating a formal layout. The formal appearance is reinforced by other elements, such as the plain type and the company name printed in full before the address.

Designed by: Vincent Sauchelli

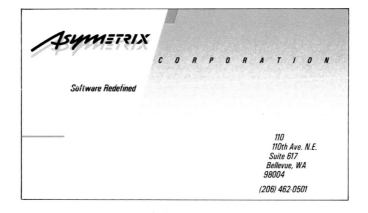

The contrasting elements, angles, and color in this informally balanced card "redefine" business card design. The faded tint is in turquoise. The rule and rectangle are in orange. The type is in black.

Designed by: Jack Anderson and Greg Walters, Hornall Anderson Design Works

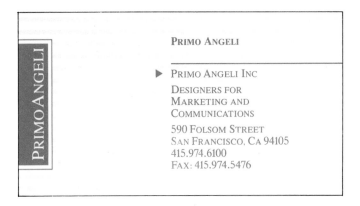

Though running type on an angle may decrease readability, with a clear, well-designed card such as Primo Angeli's, angle can be used to attract attention and provide contrast.

Designed by: Primo Angeli Inc.

The Adworks logo, contrasting in itself, works well on an angle. The *AD* and *S*, in a sans serif face, are in black; *WORK*, in a serif face, is in red.

Designed by: Jack Anderson and Julie Tanagi, Hornall Anderson Design Works

The type and art are set at a 10 degree angle, including the first name in the block. Inside the block, the signature is blue. Once the signature lines extend past the block, they become purple, the same color as the block. The first name is reversed.

Designed by: Robert Padovano, Rob-Art Graphics

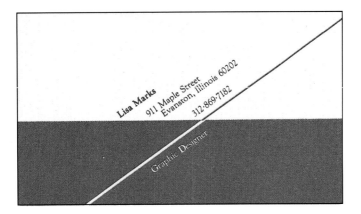

The clever use of angle and reverse type makes this an eye-catching card. The type and rule are placed at the same 145 degree angle, which increases readability.

Designed by: Lisa Marks-Ellis, Synthesis Concepts Incorporated

LA/NY MUSIC
9034 SUNSET BLVD., SUITE 101
LOS ANGELES, CA 90069
213/273-1667

The type on this card is horizontal, yet an angle effect is achieved with the right margin following the angle in the logo. LA/NY Music is a jingle production company based in both Los Angeles and New York.

Designed by: Michael Waitsman and Liane Sebastian, Synthesis Concepts Incorporated

The rounded logo blends well with the horizontal type: Each of the three curves straightens out visually by lining up with the three lines of copy.

Designed by: Mary Beth Loughlin, Synthesis Concepts Incorporated

The So Big! card is designed to look like a clothes tag. The card is hole-punched in the top left corner and string is tied through the hole.

Designed by: Modern Dog Design

FRONT ▲

▼ BACK

Two-sided cards can almost double the printing price, but they can also double the design possibilities. Here, the brush strokes printed in red and gray on the back are mirror images of and in the same position as the marks printed in light gold on the front. When the card is held up to light, the corresponding front and back marks line up, creating a single image.

Designed by: Jack Anderson and Cliff Chung, Hornall Anderson Design Works

A variety of card formats can be created through folds and die-cutting.

When having fold-over or two-sided cards printed, include a dummy with the job order to ensure that the inside or back of the card is printed in the correct position—not upside down.

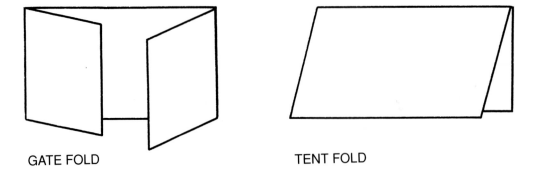

GATE FOLD   TENT FOLD

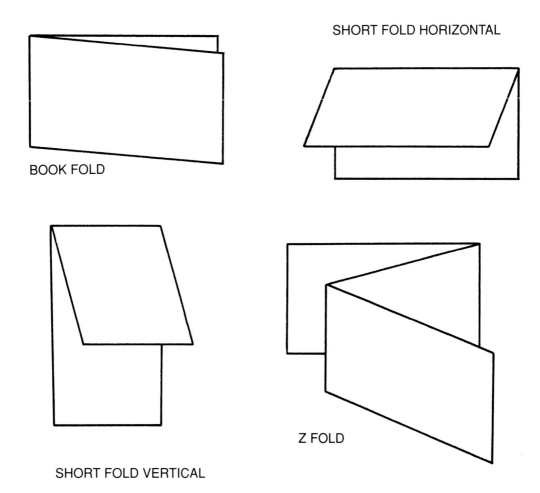

SHORT FOLD HORIZONTAL

BOOK FOLD

SHORT FOLD VERTICAL

Z FOLD

The fold on this card is on the left. The squares on the front correspond to the film's sprocket holes printed on the inside right panel. Not shown is the inside left panel, which includes the company name and address: Cole Film Service of Chicago.

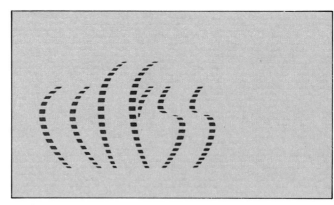

FRONT PANEL ▲

▼ INSIDE RIGHT PANEL

Designed by: Michael Waitsman and Liane Sebastian, Synthesis Concepts Incorporated

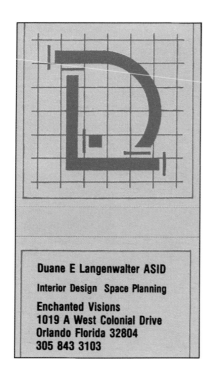

This interior designer's card is printed one side on 6 3/4 x 2 inches, folded to 2 x 3 1/2. The stock is tan laid text.

Duane E Langenwalter ASID

Interior Design Space Planning

Enchanted Visions
1019 A West Colonial Drive
Orlando Florida 32804
305 843 3103

Designed by: Duane E. Langenwalter, Thin Air

This fold-open card is a 2 3/4 inch square folded diagonally to make a triangle. This shows the inside of the card. The logotype is blind embossed on the front flap.

Designed by: Duane E. Langenwalter, Thin Air

Nonstandard sized cards literally stick out (of wallets and business card books), which can work as an advantage or disadvantage. This designer's card is 1 1/2 x 4 inches.

Designed by: R. Denzil Lee

This card from Brazil, at 1 3/4 x 3 3/4 inches, is nonstandard enough to attract attention but will still fit in most business card holders. The logo bleeds off the top.

Designed by: Neissan Monajem Design

T·H·E
TYPE

The type should reflect the company's image—which isn't to say that it must follow some stereotypical standard, such as script type for a flower shop or computer type for a computer company. Type and design are most successful when they are used creatively and originally to suggest the company's individual identity and values. Typestyle, type size, letterspacing, and line spacing can work to strengthen the image.

A note on typesetting: Numbers are the most common errors typesetters make. A thorough proofreading is essential for even the small amount of type a business card has.

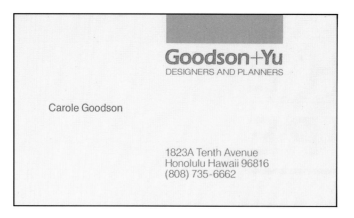

On Goodson + Yu's card, the typeface, Eras Demi, is legible and the type arrangement is readable—two requirements all type should meet.

Designed by: Goodson + Yu Design

Type can serve as a contrasting or unifying element. In the Evan Scott & Assoc. card, the sans serif and serif typeface mix creates contrast, highlighted by the narrow width of the body copy. The 1 3/4 x 3 1/2 inch size strengthens the card's vertical design.

Designed by: Evan Gross, Evan Scott & Assoc.

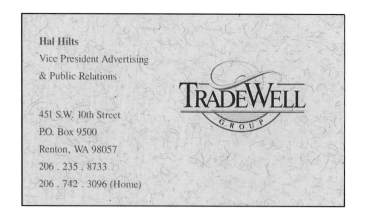

Hal Hilts
Vice President Advertising
& Public Relations

451 S.W. 10th Street
P.O. Box 9500
Renton, WA 98057
206 . 235 . 8733
206 . 742 . 3096 (Home)

Here, the same typeface for the body copy and logotype unifies the design. The logotype is Times Roman, capitals and small capitals, and the body copy is Times Roman upper and lowercase.

Designed by: Jack Anderson and Luann Bice, Hornall Anderson Design Works

The single typeface strengthens the simplicity of this card's art and design. American Typewriter Condensed works well, as all the letters—and numbers—are legible even when set in a small size.

The type, printed in gray ink, appears to be "in front" of the pink, screened dot background, giving the card a three-dimensional look.

Designed by: Goodson + Yu Design

The Seideman Company's card uses a mixture of Galliard and Galliard Italic in a variety of sizes—in caps and small caps and upper and lowercase.

Designed by: Michael M. Smit, Michael Smit & Associates Inc.

This card uses the same typeface as the Seideman card, but with a different result. Only 10 point and 8 point medium are used here, allowing the logo to dominate the card.

Designed by: Susan F. Port, Michael M. Smit & Associates Inc.

The block, sans serif face and all capital style used here ensure that the reverse type is legible. The card is over-sized at 2 1/4 x 3 1/2 inches.

Designed by: Andras Makkai

Sandra Smith, President
Practice Development, Inc.

480 Galland Building
1221 Second Avenue
Seattle, WA 98101
(206) 623-7935

Competitive Strategies for Health Professionals

Though all the type on this card is in 8 point Helvetica upper and lowercase, the company name, typeset bold, gives the card a focal point.

Designed by: John Hornall, Hornall Anderson Design Works

A block, sans serif typeface is used on this card to avoid conflicting with the logo and border, which are also included on the company's letterhead and envelopes.

Designed by: Vincent Sauchelli

Greenboam & Casey Associates

Designers

575 Eighth Avenue
New York, NY 10018
Tel. 212·564·3450

Stephanie J. Fields

Since the copy by itself must carry this card, a bold type is used: Normande Bold Italic. The employee name is contrasted not with a different typestyle but with a different color. The employee name and rule are in blue; the rest of the card is in gray.

Designed by: Robert Greenboam and Stephanie Fields, Greenboam & Casey Associates

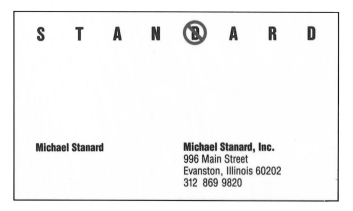

Michael Stanard, Inc. uses all caps for its logotype, and upper and lowercase for the body copy. For larger amounts of copy, upper and lowercase is usually easier to read and more informal than an all-caps style.

Designed by: Lyle Zimmerman, Michael Stanard, Inc.

```
WOOFWOOFWOOFWOOFWOOFWOOFWOOFWOOF
WOOFWOOFWOOFWOOFWOOFWOOFWOOFWOOF
WOOFWOOFCOUGHCOUGHWOOFWOOFWOOFWOOF
WOOFWOOFWOOFWOOFWOOFWOOFWOOFWOOF
WOOFWOOFWOOFWOOFWOOFWOOFWOOFWOOF
WOOFWOOFWOOFWOOFWOOFWOOFWOOFWOOF
WOOFWOOFWOOFWOOFWOOFWOOFWOOFWOOF
WOOFWOOFWOOFWOOFWOOFWOOFWOOFWOOF
WOOFWOOFWOOFWOOFWOOF      **MODERN DOG**
```

GRAPHIC DESIGN & ILLUSTRATION • 5308 BALLARD AVE. N.W.
SEATTLE, WA 98107 • (206) 789-7064

MIKE STRASSBURGER & ROBYNNE RAYE

The tight line spacing and lack of spaces between the words hide the two words near the top that are not *WOOF*. The company name is set in bold so that it stands out.

Designed by: Modern Dog Design

The sans serif typeface blends well with the logo, which symbolizes the "coming together," or synthesis, of ideas—along with an *S*. The formal all-capital style matches the formal layout.

Designed by: Michael Waitsman and Liane Sebastian, Synthesis Concepts Incorporated

Here, sans serif type is used for the English so that the English and Chinese do not conflict. The left margin of the type follows a 120 degree angle.

Designed by: Andy H. Lun, Toto Images

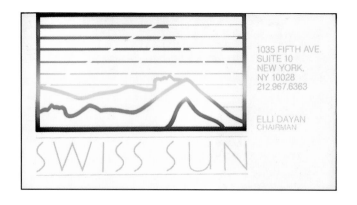

1035 FIFTH AVE.
SUITE 10
NEW YORK,
NY 10028
212.967.6363

ELLI DAYAN
CHAIRMAN

SWISS SUN

All the type on the Swiss Sun card is screened at 15 percent. The gray type is still readable, though, because it is in a block, sans serif face.

Designed by: Duk Engelhardt, DesignInk

Jodi Crupi
Advertising/Graphic Designer
25 Spring Valley Dr.
Holmdel, N.J. 07733
201-946-8329

The copy on this card is set in 6 point Serif Gothic. Many people—without their glasses—cannot read type smaller than 8 point, especially type with a small x-height. Clear type and a clean layout, however, can help improve readability.

Designed by: Jodi Crupi

When copy must stretch a certain length, words can be added, type size increased, or letterspacing expanded. The latter method is employed here so that all the copy lines are justified inside the 8 1/2 pica border.

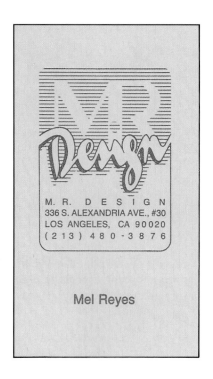

Designed by: M.R. Design

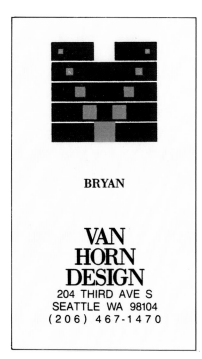

BRYAN

VAN
HORN
DESIGN

204 THIRD AVE S
SEATTLE WA 98104
(206) 467-1470

Here, positive and negative letterspacing is used in the body copy for a specific design purpose. The body copy, in the shape of a pyramid, matches the inverted pyramid, or *V*, formed by the squares in the art above.

Designed by: Cliff Chung, Hornall Anderson Design Works

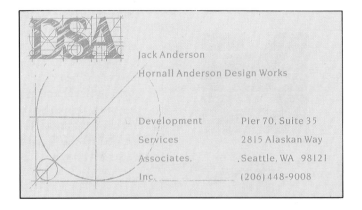

The positive letterspacing and open line spacing make the 7 point type on this card more readable. The background art is in brown, as are the address and phone number.

Designed by: Jack Anderson, Juliet Shen, and Heidi Hatlestad, Hornall Anderson Design Works

Letterspacing can be adjusted for better readability, for aesthetics, or so that type fills a certain length. The open letterspacing on Jim Laser's card serves all three purposes. The spaced body copy matches the logotype, which is blind embossed over the purple shading.

Designed by: Jack Anderson and Cliff Chung, Hornall Anderson Design Works

Line spacing should be increased when the type is bold, the type has long ascenders and descenders, or the copy runs the whole width of the card.

The body copy on this card is 14 point with 8 point line spacing, enhancing the vertical design.

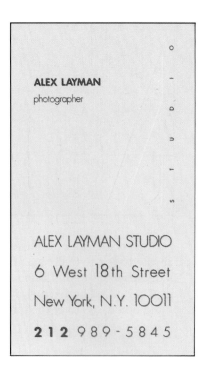

Designed by: Dana Shimizu

ABRAMS DESIGN GROUP

100 VIEW STREET, STE. 203

MOUNTAIN VIEW, CA 94041

415.964.2388

Colleen Abrams

On this designer's card, white space is inserted in the type through positive letterspacing in the company name and open line spacing in the address.

Designed by: Abrams Design Group

The leading for the body copy is standard 2 point line spacing; however, the rules seem to open up the space and separate the copy lines. Letterspacing is adjusted so that all lines extend to 5 1/2 picas.

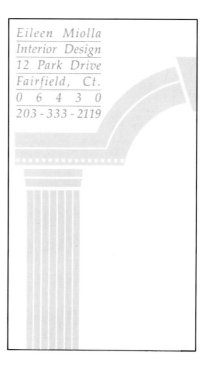

Eileen Miolla
Interior Design
12 Park Drive
Fairfield, Ct.
0 6 4 3 0
203 - 333 - 2119

Designed by: Port Miolla

T·H·E
PAPER
& INK

Black ink on white stock may be the most readable color combination, though not necessarily the most interesting. Finding the happy medium between being readable and appealing is the challenge of selecting ink and paper color.

But being pleasing to the eye is not the only requirement cards must meet. Because they are handled so much, business cards must be pleasing to the touch, which makes the weight and finish of the paper an important consideration also.

ARTESANIA INC.
274 Columbus Ave. NYC, NY 10023   212.769.9377

Text cover paper is a popular choice for business cards as it offers a wide selection of both finishes and colors. Textures of uncoated cover stock include antique, felt, laid, linen, vellum, and wove. The Artesania card is printed on 80 lb. ivory laid.

Designed by: Evan Gross, Evan Scott & Assoc.

The most common text cover weights for business cards are 65 and 80 lb.

The Ultimo card is printed on 65 lb. light gold parchment cover. The stock has an antique appearance that complements the art.

Designed by: Clare Ultimo

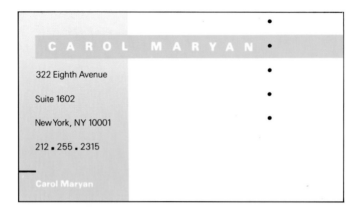

Coated stock is available in 60, 80, and 100 lb. weights and in mostly white and off-white. Popular finishes are dull, gloss, and matte.

This card is printed on a glossy coated stock, allowing for clean, smooth printing. Glare is hardly a factor on business cards since the amount of type is so small.

Designed by: Tom Dolle Design

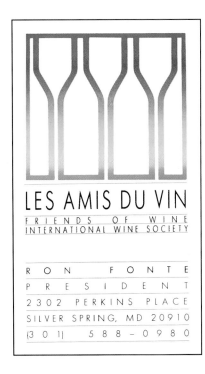

Images are sharper and colors more brilliant on coated stock since the ink dries on the surface of the coated paper rather than being absorbed into it, as in the case of uncoated stock.

The full-color logo on this card, printed on white coated stock, utilizes the shape of the wine bottle and wine glass.

Designed by: Duk Engelhardt, DesignInk

This full-color photograph is reproduced well on coated cover. The smooth stock allows for the use of a tighter halftone screen.

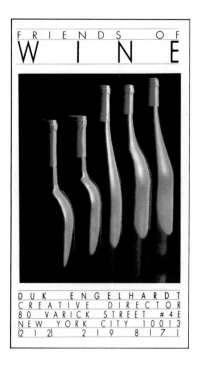

Designed by: Duk Engelhardt, DesignInk

■

Arizona State University

West Campus

2636 W. Montebello Avenue
Phoenix, Arizona 85017

Susan Bobbitt Nolen, Ph.D.
Education and Human Services Faculty
602/246-6557

The color of the business card stock should coordinate with the letterhead, being either a complementary color or the same color. Obtaining the exact same color is often difficult, however, since paper color may vary slightly from cover to text.

This card is printed on 65 lb. ivory laid cover, with the letterhead on 24 lb. ivory laid text. Variances in lighter colored stock are less apparent.

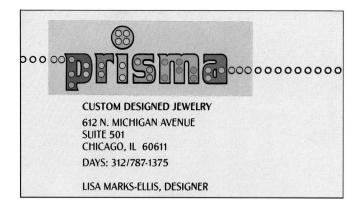

CUSTOM DESIGNED JEWELRY

612 N. MICHIGAN AVENUE
SUITE 501
CHICAGO, IL 60611
DAYS: 312/787-1375

LISA MARKS-ELLIS, DESIGNER

A full-color label is placed on this card, which is printed on duplex linen stock. The front of the card is light gray, the back is dark gray.

The jewelry made by Prisma is designed from buttons.

Designed by: Lisa Marks-Ellis and Liane Sebastian, Synthesis Concepts Incorporated

With gray and white ink and mauve stock, this card breaks the general rule of having the color in the ink rather than in the paper. Nevertheless, the card is attractive and readable. The mauve stock gives the card an elegant, artistic look.

Designed by: Jack Anderson and Juliet Shen, Hornall Anderson Design Works

DIVISION OF THE UNISOURCE CORP.
AN ALCO STANDARD COMPANY

CANDY WILLS
Manager

7700 North 67th Avenue
Glendale, AZ 85301
(602) 937-2703

The Paper Plus card is printed on 65 lb. bright white smooth cover. With a white background, art and type are more clear. A disadvantage of white stock is that though it may start out looking cleaner, it seems to get dirtier faster.

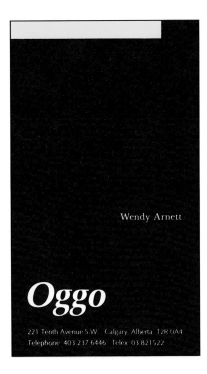

A yellow rectangle and embossed square contribute to the uniqueness of this reverse card. The disadvantage of an all black card is that it shows wear and tear more quickly.

Designed by: Corporate Communications Specialists

The gray background is softer than 100 percent black yet still dark enough for reverse type to be read easily. Dal Barone is an Italian restaurant.

Designed by: Duk Engelhardt, DesignInk

A gray background is printed on this coated stock. *Classical Guitarist* and the rules are reversed; the rest of the type is printed in maroon. The result is an elegant, "classical" look.

Designed by: Lisa Marks-Ellis, Synthesis Concepts Incorporated

The background ink on this white coated stock is a rich, solid maroon. The logo and rules are printed in silver, and the address is left as a reverse.

Especially on cards with large, solid areas of ink, sufficient drying time must be allowed to avoid offsetting, or having the backs of the cards imprinted with the front image.

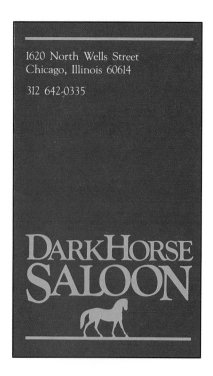

Designed by: Michael Stanard, Inc.

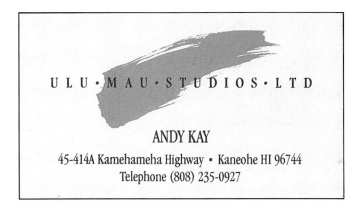

The color of the brushstroke on the Ulu Mau Studios card differs for each employee. The body copy and logotype are gray on all the cards.

Designed by: Goodson + Yu Design

The Children's Foundation

Patricia Barber

The Children's Foundation of St. Louis, Incorporated
3532 Laclede Avenue ▪ St. Louis, Missouri 63103
314-388-5399 ▪ 314-367-2524

The employee name and the square bullets in the address are in gray with the rest of the card in maroon.

When a large amount of company cards are to be printed first with employee names to be imprinted later, it is often difficult to perfectly match inks. Having the employee names printed in an entirely different color solves the problem.

Designed by: Susan F. Port, Michael M. Smit & Associates Inc.

Here, different line screens and color mixing create a variety of colors with only two colors of ink. The diagonal screened lines running behind the type start in green at the lower right corner and slowly fade to yellow as they proceed up the card.

Designed by: Jack Anderson and Juliet Shen, Hornall Anderson Design Works

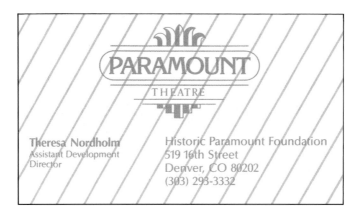

Two contrasting ink colors help to make this design a success. The diagonal rules are printed in light brown and the type is in green. The green ink is bold enough so that it shows through clearly where the rules intersect with the type.

Designed by: Unit 1, Inc.

Bright, spring colors are used in the ink on this card. The paper is a bright yellow linen.

Designed by: Gene Russell, Bay East Graphics

We deliver for you!

The Daily News-Tribune
426 Second Street
LaSalle, Illinois 61301
815/223-3200

Robert F. Vickrey
Vice President
Sales and Marketing

NewsTribune

Gray ink, as opposed to black ink, can make a card look friendlier or more sophisticated. The gray ink softens this bold type without reducing the logo's impact.

Designed by: Michael Stanard, Inc.

LAUREATE DESIGN GROUP INK LTD./DBA.

DESIGNINK

**DUK
ENGELHARDT**
PRESIDENT

80 VARICK STREET
NEW YORK NY 10013
(212)941-0965

INK is printed in metallic silver with *DESIGN* in black, emphasizing the two words that make up the company name. With the metallic ink, coated stock is used for better results.

Designed by: Duk Engelhardt, DesignInk

To make the color separations and printing easier on this card, the black type and rules are printed over the yellow ink inside the designs. The black ink is opaque enough not to allow the yellow background to show through.

Designed by: Interstate

ROCKET

SURFWEAR
USA

ROCKETWEAR USA, INC.
660 MISSION STREET, 4TH FLOOR
SAN FRANCISCO, CA 94105
(415) 495-5515

The registration on this card is tight, but the black outlines and shadows around the type separate the red lettering from the blue background so that the two colors cannot mix to make purple.

Design by: Mark Oliver Inc.

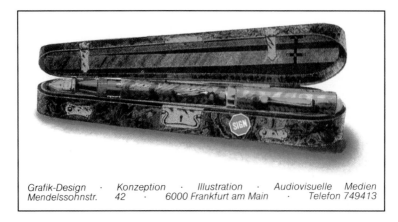

Grafik-Design · Konzeption · Illustration · Audiovisuelle Medien
Mendelssohnstr. 42 · 6000 Frankfurt am Main · Telefon 749413

Studio Sign in West Germany prints many different full-color and limited-color cards. The oversized, uniquely illustrated cards display a fine sample of the company's work. All of the illustrations on the cards include the company's red SIGN logo.

Designed by: Karl W. Henschel, Studio Sign

Grafik-Design · Konzeption · Illustration
Audiovisuelle Medien · Mendelssohnstr. 42
6000 Frankfurt am Main · Telefon 749413

Grafik-Design · Konzeption · Illustration
Audiovisuelle Medien · Mendelssohnstr. 42
6000 Frankfurt am Main · Telefon 749413

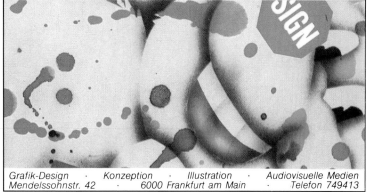

Grafik-Design · Konzeption · Illustration · Audiovisuelle Medien
Mendelssohnstr. 42 · 6000 Frankfurt am Main · Telefon 749413

RENTON MITCHELL

Santa Ynez Valley Printing & Lithography

175 INDUSTRIAL WAY, BUELLTON, CA 93427 (805) 688-2285

This card shows rather than tells the company's full-color capabilities. The tree is in full color, changing from blue on the left to green to yellow to orange to red.

Designed by: Mark Oliver Inc.

S·P·E·C·I·A·L
PROCESSES

Interest and allure can be added to the business card through the use of a variety of special printing and finishing processes, including embossing, blind embossing, foil stamping, and die-cutting.

With careful planning, these techniques can help to create a visual and tactile impression that's positive and long-lasting.

The embossing on this card makes the robin's egg appear three-dimensional. The shadow under the blue embossed egg heightens the three-dimensional effect.

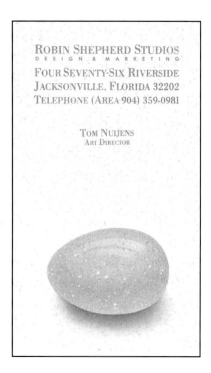

Designed by: Tom Nuijens, Robin Shepherd Studios

Here, multi-level embossing is used, giving the look of real wheat. The complete logo is embossed. This is a fold-open card with addresses of the four California locations printed on the inside.

Designed by: Primo Angeli and John Lodge, Primo Angeli Inc.

The background of this logo, rather than the logo itself, is foil embossed in silver. The letters *MSSA* are left unprinted.

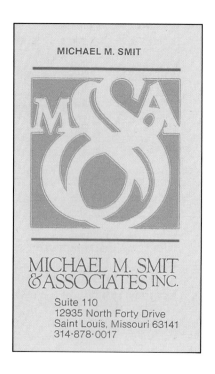

Designed by: Michael M. Smit, Michael M. Smit & Associates Inc.

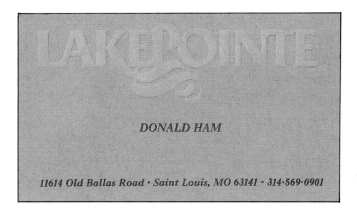

The logo on this card is blind embossed—no ink is printed on the embossed area. When type or art is to be blind embossed, it can be larger than if it were printed in solid, dark ink.

Designed by: Michael M. Smit, Michael M. Smit & Associates Inc.

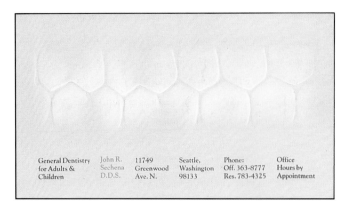

General Dentistry for Adults & Children	John R. Sechena D.D.S.	11749 Greenwood Ave. N.	Seattle, Washington 98133	Phone: Off. 363-8777 Res. 783-4325	Office Hours by Appointment

A set of molars and bicuspids are embossed on this dentist's card. At the "gums," the embossed teeth blend smoothly into the non-embossed area.

Designed by: Jack Anderson, Hornall Anderson Design Works

ANDY LUN
DESIGN CONSULTANT

倫

435 MIDWAY AVENUE
FANWOOD, NEW JERSEY
07023
201-889-7356

Heavy, uncoated stock is best for embossing. Andy Lun's card is printed on 80 lb. white bristol cover. The embossed logo, here printed in black, stands for the designer's last name.

Designed by: Andy Lun, Toto Images

The diacritical marks, punctuation marks, the rule, and the descending dots on this card are foil stamped in silver. In foil stamping, metallic or pigmented foil is applied with a metal die through heat and pressure. Foil stamping can be combined with embossing or, as in this case, used by itself.

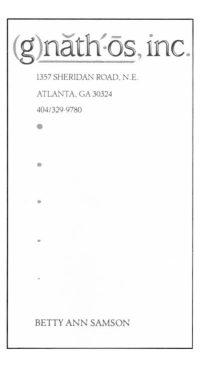

Designed by: Michael Waitsman and Mary Beth Loughlin, Synthesis Concepts Incorporated

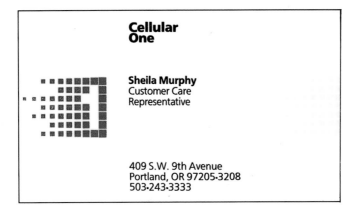

**Cellular
One**

Sheila Murphy
Customer Care
Representative

409 S.W. 9th Avenue
Portland, OR 97205-3208
503·243·3333

Many different colors and types of foils are available. Here, the squares and the number one logo on the left are foil stamped in metallic silver with two halftone graduated screens printed in red on top.

Designed by: Jack Anderson and Raymond Terada, Hornall Anderson Design Works

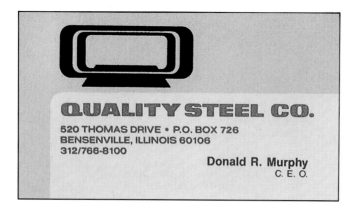

The logo on this card is foil stamped in a black matte ink.
A fine, light screen is printed in gray behind the logo.

Designed by: Michael Waitsman and Liane Sebastian,
Synthesis Concepts Incorporated

Ultra Stamping and Assembly, Inc.
4838 Colt Road
Rockford, Illinois 61109

815/874-9888

Jim Pettit
President

Here, the letters *USA* are die-cut on a 90 degree angle. The typestyle of the logo is effective with this finishing process.

Designed by: Michael Stanard, Inc.

This fold-open card for a design company in Berlin has thin slats die-cut on the front. The gray and red rules on the inside panel show through. The card opens like a book and is scored to provide a clean, smooth fold.

Designed by:
Headline Werbung

H E A D L | N E

WERBUNG |

Nicolaistraße 48 a
1000 Berlin 46
Telefon: 0 30 · 7 71 94 00

Irene Grünmeier
Wolfgang Müßig

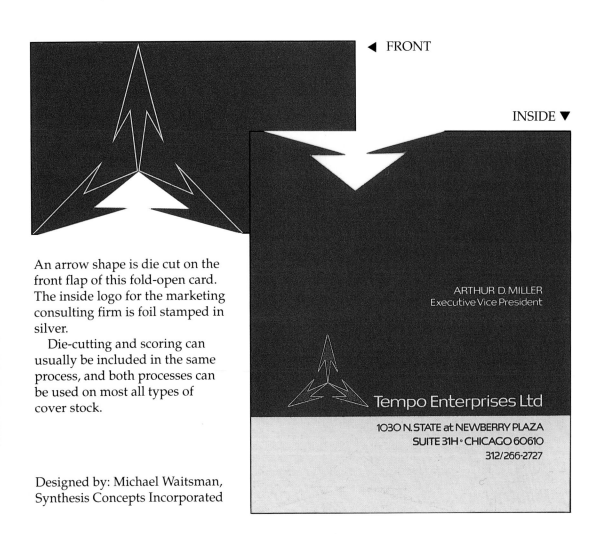

◀ FRONT

INSIDE ▼

ARTHUR D. MILLER
Executive Vice President

Tempo Enterprises Ltd

1030 N. STATE at NEWBERRY PLAZA
SUITE 31H • CHICAGO 60610
312/266-2727

An arrow shape is die cut on the front flap of this fold-open card. The inside logo for the marketing consulting firm is foil stamped in silver.

Die-cutting and scoring can usually be included in the same process, and both processes can be used on most all types of cover stock.

Designed by: Michael Waitsman, Synthesis Concepts Incorporated

An open door is an appropriate symbol for this business—an interior decorating company. A 1 1/2 x 7 inches rectangle opens up on this card. Three sides of the "door" are die-cut. The left side, or hinged side, is scored.

Designed by:
Wilkins & Peterson

SUSAN
WELLS
INTERI(INC)RS

10801 Main Street
Suite 200
Bellevue, WA 98004
(206) 454-9290

Susan Wells

Biddulphland's card is die-cut in the shape that has become a part of the company's trademark. The address, phone number, and employee's name are printed on the back of the card.

Steel-die engraving is used on this card. The costly process produces an embossed printed surface, with a slightly indented impression on the back of the card.

The Bolling & Finke card is slightly oversized and has rounded corners.

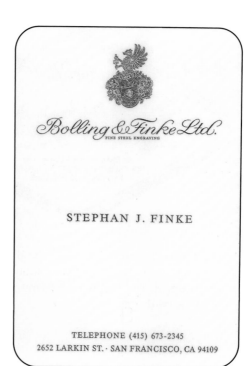

Designed by:
Stephan J. Finke

ACE GRAPHICS
4708 Belmont Road
Downers Grove, IL 60515

RODNEY KRANZ
312/969-3997

Ace Graphics' card is laminated and the corners rounded, making the card appear more like a playing card. The front of the card is in black ink. The back is in blue.

Designed by: Michael Stanard, Inc.

C·A·R·D
INDEX

D·E·S·I·G·N·E·R·S

Abrams Design Group
See Page 101

Primo Angeli Inc.
Art Director: Primo Angeli
See Page 64

Bay East Graphics
See Page 10

Martha A. Bogdanoff
See Page 20

Bolling & Finke Ltd.
See Page 144

Bowen Designs
Toronto, Ontario, Canada

Copeland Design, Incorporated
See Page 44

Corporate Communications Specialists
Calgary, Alberta, Canada

Sandy Cowen Agency Inc.
See Page 13

Creative Edge Inc.
See Page 51

Jodi Crupi
See Page 95

DesignInk
See Page 123

Tom Dolle Design
55 W. 45th Street, #5
New York, NY 10036

Thom Dower
See Page 50

General Binding Corporation
See Page 34

Goodson + Yu Design
Designers: Carole Goodson
and Roger Yu
See Page 80

Graphics One
Route 2, Box 202
Menomonie, WI 54751

Greenboam & Casey Associates
See Page 89

Group 243 Inc.
1410 Woodridge Ave.
Ann Arbor, MI 48105

Headline Werbung
See Page 140

Hornall Anderson Design Works
411 First Ave., S.
Seattle, WA 98104

Image Design Advertising Studio
Suite 210 Sun Tower
1550 Bedford Highway
Bedford, Nova Scotia B4A 1E6

Inside Mechanicals
See Page 23

Interstate
See Page 124

George Kavanagh
See Page 35

R. Denzil Lee
See Page 77

LMG Communications
See Page 21

Andras Makkai
See Page 86

Modern Dog Design
See Page 91

M.R. Design
See Page 96

Neissan Monajem Design
See Page 78

Mark Oliver Inc.
1 West Victoria
Santa Barbara, CA 93101

Pappas & MacDonnell
528 Clinton Avenue
Bridgeport, CT 06605

Port Miolla
See Page 45

Potts & Plans
Route 10, Box 380
Waco, TX 76708

Rob-Art Graphics
538 82nd Street
Brooklyn, NY 11209

Salpeter Paganucci, Inc.
142 E. 37th Street
New York, NY 10016

Vincent Sauchelli
1007 Whittier Ave.
New Hyde Park, NY 11040

Evan Scott & Assoc.
See Page 81

Robin Shepherd Studio
See Page 25 or 130

Dana Shimizu
181 7th Ave., #6-B
New York, NY 10011

Michael M. Smit & Associates Inc.
See Page 132

Susan Spivack Graphic Design
See Page 40

Michael Stanard, Inc.
See Page 90

Studio Sign
See Pages 126 and 127

Synthesis Concepts Incorporated
See Page 92

Thin Air
See Page 76

Toto Images
396 Broadway, Suite 600-A
New York, NY 10013

Claire Ultimo
See Page 105

Ulu Mau Studios
See Page 117

Unit 1, Inc.
Art Director: Chuck Danford
See Page 55

Wilkins & Peterson
1510 Alaskan Way
Seattle, WA 98101-1514